MUFFINS

MUFFINS

40 TANTALIZING RECIPES FOR TASTY MUFFINS

LOVE FOOD

First published in 2009

Love Food ® is an imprint of Parragon Books Ltd

Parragon
Queen Street House
4 Queen Street
Bath BA1 1HE, UK

ISBN: 978-1-4075-6837-9

Printed in China

Design concept by Fiona Roberts
Produced by Ivy Contract Ltd

Notes for the Reader
This book uses both metric and imperial measurements. Follow the same units of
measurement throughout; do not mix metric and imperial. All spoon measurements are
level: teaspoons are assumed to be 5 ml and tablespoons are assumed to be 15 ml.
Unless otherwise stated, milk is assumed to be full fat, eggs and individual vegetables
such as potatoes are medium, and pepper is freshly ground black pepper. Recipes using
raw or very lightly cooked eggs should be avoided by infants, the elderly, pregnant women,
convalescents and anyone suffering from an illness. The times given are an approximate
guide only.

Picture acknowledgement
Ivy Contract would like to thank Simon Jauncey/Stone/Getty Images for permission to
reproduce copyright material for the endpapers.

Introduction

There's something so satisfying about baking a batch of muffins. Perhaps it's because they're so quick and easy to make, because there are so many delicious variations, from fresh fruit to chocolate, or simply because they look and smell so wonderfully appetizing. Even so, the pleasure of making them is secondary to the bliss of biting into the warm, melt-in-the-mouth texture of a freshly baked muffin.

Everyone loves muffins but you'd probably never get them to agree on which type is the best, with some voting for spicy apple muffins, others for savoury cheese and probably quite a lot for chocolate. So it's just as well that this book contains a comprehensive collection of perennially popular recipes. In addition, it also offers some clever new ideas for both sweet and savoury treats.

The recipes are divided into four chapters, making it easy to find just the right one. Sweet Indulgences are everyday family bakes, often made with store-cupboard ingredients. Healthy Choices provides some smart ideas for those trying to reduce their intake of fat and sugar but who still have a sweet tooth. Savoury Muffins is full of delicious and unusual lunchtime snacks and perfect picnic suggestions, while the recipes in Muffins for Special Occasions provide both the means and excuse for a party.

There's nothing like a warm muffin with a cup of coffee during a well-earned mid-morning break or as a tasty snack for ravenous children when they come home from school. This chapter is packed with family favourites — and, perhaps a few surprises — for just such occasions. However, beware — if news of your baking prowess gets round, you may find a whole class of children dropping in on their way home.

Fresh and dried fruit, warm spices, chopped nuts and, of course, chocolate are among the featured flavours. There are recipes for popular, classic combinations, such as Apple and Cinnamon Muffins and Chocolate Orange Muffins as well as for some more unusual mixtures that you might like to try, such as Nectarine and Banana Muffins and Lime and Poppy Seed Muffins.

SWEET INDULGENCES

All these recipes are very quick and easy, yet taste fabulous. It's simplicity itself to rustle up a batch for breakfast or when unexpected guests arrive. They cook in no time at all and you don't have to wait for them to cool because there are no extra toppings to spread. In any case, they smell so appetizing and taste so delicious when freshly baked that it would be virtually impossible to prevent the family from instantly indulging themselves.

If by any strange chance these muffins are not all scoffed instantly, you can store them in an airtight container. They will keep for a day or two, but are always much better eaten on the day they are baked, whether warm or cold.

MAKES 12

3 tbsp soft margarine

200 g/7 oz caster sugar

2 large eggs

150 ml/5 fl oz full-fat natural yogurt

5 tbsp milk

280 g/10 oz plain flour

1 tsp bicarbonate of soda

175 g/6 oz plain chocolate chips

Chocolate Chip Muffins

The mixture can also be used to make 6 large or 24 mini muffins. Bake mini muffins for 10 minutes and large ones for 25 minutes or both until springy to the touch.

• Preheat the oven to 200°C/400°F/Gas Mark 6. Line a muffin tin with 12 paper cases.

• Place the margarine and sugar in a mixing bowl and beat with a wooden spoon until light and fluffy. Beat in the eggs, yogurt and milk until combined.

• Sift the flour and bicarbonate of soda into the mixture. Stir until just blended.

• Stir in the chocolate chips, then divide the mixture between the paper cases (they should be about two-thirds full) and bake in the oven for 20 minutes or until risen and golden. Remove the muffins from the oven and leave to cool in the tin for 5 minutes, then put them on a wire rack to cool completely.

MAKES 6

85 g/3 oz plain wholemeal flour

70 g/2½ oz plain white flour

1½ tsp baking powder

pinch of salt

1 tsp ground cinnamon

40 g/1½ oz golden caster sugar

2 small eating apples, peeled, cored
   and finely chopped

125 ml/4 fl oz milk

1 egg, beaten

55 g/2 oz butter, melted

TOPPING

12 brown sugar lumps, coarsely
   crushed

½ tsp ground cinnamon

Apple and Cinnamon Muffins

These spicy muffins are quick and easy to make with a few store cupboard ingredients and two small apples. The crunchy sugar topping is a treat.

• Preheat the oven to 200°C/400°F/Gas Mark 6. Place 6 muffin paper cases in a muffin tin.

• Sift together both the flours, the baking powder, salt and cinnamon into a large bowl and stir in the sugar and chopped apples. Place the milk, egg and butter in a separate bowl and mix. Add the wet ingredients to the dry ingredients and gently stir until just combined.

• Divide the mixture between the paper cases (they should be about two-thirds full). To make the topping, mix together the crushed sugar lumps and cinnamon and sprinkle over the muffins. Bake in the oven for 20–25 minutes or until risen and golden. Remove the muffins from the oven and serve them warm or put them on a wire rack and leave to cool.

MAKES 12
200 g/7 oz plain flour
25 g/1 oz cocoa powder, plus extra
    for dusting
1 tbsp baking powder
1 tsp ground cinnamon
115 g/4 oz golden
caster sugar

185 g/6½ oz white chocolate,
    broken into pieces
2 eggs
100 ml/3½ fl oz sunflower oil
225 ml/8 fl oz milk

Double Chocolate Muffins

When stirring the muffin batter together, do not overstir or the muffins will be tough. The batter should be quite lumpy.

• Preheat the oven to 200°C/400°F/Gas Mark 6. Line a 12-cup muffin tin with muffin paper cases.

• Sift the flour, cocoa, baking powder and cinnamon into a large mixing bowl. Stir in the sugar and 125 g/4½ oz of the white chocolate.

• Place the eggs and oil in a separate bowl and whisk until frothy, then gradually whisk in the milk. Stir into the dry ingredients until just blended. Divide the mixture between the paper cases (they should be about two-thirds full). Bake in the oven for 20 minutes or until well risen and springy to the touch. Remove the muffins from the oven, leave to cool in the tin for 2 minutes, then remove them and put them on a wire rack to cool completely.

• Melt the remaining white chocolate in a heatproof bowl set over a saucepan of gently simmering water until melted and spread over the top of the muffins. Leave to set, then dust the tops with a little cocoa and serve.

MAKES 8

150 g/5½ oz plain flour

1½ tsp baking powder

pinch of salt

60 g/2¼ oz golden caster sugar

115 g/4 oz cup pecan nuts, coarsely
   chopped

2 large ripe bananas, mashed

5 tbsp milk

2 tbsp butter, melted

1 egg, beaten

½ tsp vanilla essence

Banana Pecan Muffins

This is a good way of
using up ripe bananas.
Try hazelnuts or walnuts
instead of pecan nuts.

• Preheat the oven to 190°C/375°F/Gas Mark 5. Place 8 muffin paper cases in a muffin tin.

• Sift the flour, baking powder and salt into a bowl, add the sugar and pecan nuts and stir to combine.

• Put the mashed bananas, milk, butter, egg and vanilla essence in another bowl and mix together. Add the wet ingredients to the dry ingredients and gently stir until just combined.

• Divide the mixture between the paper cases (they should be about two-thirds full) and bake in the oven for 20–25 minutes or until risen and golden. Remove the muffins from the oven and put them on a wire rack to cool.

MAKES 12
250 g/9 oz plain flour
4 tsp baking powder
85 g/3 oz caster sugar
6 tbsp crunchy peanut butter
1 egg, beaten

55 g/2 oz butter, melted
175 ml/6 fl oz milk
150 g/5½ oz vanilla fudge, cut into
    small pieces
3 tbsp coarsely chopped unsalted
    peanuts

Fudge Nut Muffins

Chewy pieces of fudge give these muffins a lovely texture and contrast with the crunchiness of the nuts. Store in airtight containers.

• Preheat the oven to 200°C/400°F/Gas Mark 6. Line a 12-cup muffin tin with muffin paper cases.
• Sift the flour and baking powder into a bowl. Stir in the caster sugar. Add the peanut butter and stir until the mixture resembles breadcrumbs.
• Place the egg, butter and milk in a separate bowl and beat until blended, then stir into the dry ingredients until just blended. Lightly stir in the fudge pieces. Spoon the mixture into the muffin cases.
• Sprinkle the chopped peanuts on top and bake in the oven for 20–25 minutes or until well risen and firm to the touch. Remove the muffins from the oven and leave to cool for 2 minutes, then put them on a wire rack to cool completely.

MAKES 8–10

sunflower oil, for oiling

125 g/4½ oz self-raising flour

125 g/4½ oz self-raising
wholemeal flour

25 g/1 oz ground almonds

55 g/2 oz soft brown sugar

rind and juice of 1 orange

175 g/6 oz cream cheese

2 eggs

55 g/2 oz plain chocolate chips

Chocolate Orange Muffins

These muffins are a favourite with children of all ages. They are best served warm and are particularly good for breakfast.

• Preheat the oven to 190°C/375°F/Gas Mark 5. Thoroughly oil the muffin tins.

• Sift the flours into a mixing bowl and add the ground almonds and sugar.

• Mix together the orange rind and juice, the cream cheese and the eggs in a separate bowl. Make a well in the centre of the flour mixture and stir in the liquid, then add the chocolate chips. Beat the mixture well to combine all the ingredients.

• Divide the mixture between the muffin tins (they should be about two-thirds full).

• Bake in the oven for 20–25 minutes or until well risen and golden brown.

• Remove the muffins from the oven and leave to cool slightly on a wire rack, but eat them as fresh as possible.

MAKES 12
100 ml/3½ fl oz vegetable oil, plus
    extra for oiling (if using)
250 g/9 oz plain flour
1 tsp bicarbonate of soda
¼ tsp salt
¼ tsp mixed spice
100 g/3½ oz caster sugar
75 g/2¾ oz almonds, chopped

175 g/6 oz ripe nectarine, peeled and
    chopped
1 ripe banana, peeled and sliced
2 eggs
90 ml/3¼ fl oz thick Greek-style
    natural or banana-flavoured yogurt
1 tsp almond essence

Nectarine and Banana Muffins

To add a delicious crunchy topping to these muffins, put 3 tablespoons demerara sugar and 1 teaspoon mixed spice in a small bowl and mix together well. Just before transferring the muffins to the oven, sprinkle some of the spiced sugar over each muffin.

• Preheat the oven to 200°C/400°F/Gas Mark 6. Oil a 12-cup muffin tin with vegetable oil, or line it with muffin paper cases.
• Sift the flour, bicarbonate of soda, salt and mixed spice into a mixing bowl. Then add the caster sugar and chopped almonds and stir together.
• In a separate large bowl, mash together the chopped nectarine and banana, then stir in the eggs, remaining vegetable oil, yogurt and almond essence. Add the mashed fruit mixture to the flour mixture and then gently stir together until just combined. Do not over-stir the mixture – it is fine for it to be a little lumpy.
• Divide the mixture between the 12 cups in the muffin tin or the paper cases (they should be about two-thirds full). Transfer to the oven and bake for about 20 minutes or until risen and golden. Remove the muffins from the oven and serve warm, or put them on a wire rack and leave to cool.

MAKES 12

175 ml/6 fl oz vegetable oil, plus extra
   for oiling (if using)

215 g/7½ oz plain flour

1 tsp baking powder

½ tsp salt

225 g/8 oz caster sugar

1 egg

1 egg white

150 ml/5 fl oz milk

1 tbsp lime juice

1 tbsp grated lime rind

2 tsp poppy seeds

TO DECORATE

2 tsp grated lime rind

1–2 tsp poppy seeds

Lime and Poppy Seed Muffins

To ring the changes, why not try varying the flavour? You can substitute the same quantity of lemon juice and rind for the lime, or for a milder flavour, use the same quantity of orange juice and rind instead of the lime.

• Preheat the oven to 190°C/375°F/Gas Mark 5. Oil a 12-cup muffin tin with vegetable oil, or line it with muffin paper cases.

• Sift the flour, baking powder and salt into a mixing bowl. Then add the caster sugar and stir together.

• In a separate bowl, whisk together the egg, egg white, remaining vegetable oil and the milk, then stir in the lime juice and grated lime rind. Add the egg mixture to the flour mixture, then add the poppy seeds and gently stir together. Do not over-stir the mixture – it is fine for it to be a little lumpy.

• Divide the mixture between the 12 cups in the muffin tin or the paper cases (they should be about two-thirds full). Sprinkle over grated lime rind and poppy seeds to decorate, then bake in the oven for about 25 minutes or until risen and golden. Remove the muffins from the oven and serve warm, or put them on a wire rack and leave to cool.

MAKES 12

2 tbsp vegetable oil, plus extra for
    oiling (if using)

250 g/9 oz plain flour

1 tsp bicarbonate of soda

½ tsp salt

200 g/7 oz demerara sugar

100 g/3½ oz dried figs, chopped

150 g/5½ oz almonds, chopped

225 ml/8 fl oz water

1 tsp almond essence

2 tbsp chopped almonds, to decorate

Fig and Almond Muffins

You can replace the dried figs with the same quantity of ready-to-eat dried dates or apricots. And why not try replacing the almonds with the same quantity of walnuts or pecan nuts? Try your own combinations to vary the flavour.

• Preheat the oven to 190°C/375°F/Gas Mark 5. Oil a 12-cup muffin tin with vegetable oil, or line it with muffin paper cases.

• Sift the flour, bicarbonate of soda and salt into a mixing bowl. Then add the demerara sugar and stir together.

• In a separate bowl, mix together the figs, almonds and remaining vegetable oil. Then stir in the water and almond essence. Add the fruit and nut mixture to the flour mixture and gently stir together. Do not over-stir — it is fine for it to be a little lumpy.

• Divide the mixture between the 12 cups in the muffin tin or the paper cases (they should be about two-thirds full), then sprinkle over the remaining chopped almonds to decorate. Transfer to the oven and bake for about 25 minutes or until risen and golden. Remove the muffins from the oven and serve warm, or put them on a wire rack and leave to cool.

MAKES 12

100 g/3½ oz butter, softened

125 g/4½ oz caster sugar

100 g/3½ oz dark muscovado sugar

2 eggs

150 ml/5 fl oz soured cream

5 tbsp milk

250 g/9 oz plain flour

1 tsp bicarbonate of soda

2 tbsp cocoa powder

1 tsp mixed spice

190 g/6½ oz dark chocolate chips

Spiced Chocolate Muffins

You can replace the mixed spice with ground cinnamon or with a mixture of equal parts nutmeg and cloves.

• Preheat the oven to 190°C/375°F/Gas Mark 5. Line a 12-cup muffin tin with paper cases.

• Put the butter, caster sugar and dark muscovado sugar into a bowl and beat well. Beat in the eggs, cream and milk until thoroughly mixed. Sift the flour, bicarbonate of soda, cocoa powder and mixed spice into a separate bowl and stir into the mixture. Add the chocolate chips and mix well. Divide the mixture between the paper cases (they should be about two-thirds full). Bake in the oven for 25–30 minutes.

• Remove from the oven and leave to cool for 10 minutes. Put them on a wire rack and leave to cool completely. Store in an airtight container until required.

There's no reason why just because you're counting the calories or trying to follow a healthy diet you should miss out on the pleasures of home-baked treats. The judicious use of low-fat ingredients and the imaginative substitution of the natural sweetness of fruit for added refined sugar are just two of the ways suggested for making healthy choices.

The recipes in this chapter are the proof that being careful about using healthier ingredients doesn't in any way sacrifice flavour or variety. Indeed, you could serve any of this fabulous batch of muffins to family and friends and they wouldn't even be able to tell the difference. There's even a recipe for Sugarless Chocolate Muffins (see page 42), so you can spoil yourself without spoiling your good dietary intentions.

HEALTHY CHOICES

While reducing levels of fats and sugars in their diet is among the main concerns of people aiming for a healthier lifestyle, the recipes in this chapter also address other considerations. Intolerance to dairy products is on the increase and such ingredients are also thought to aggravate other conditions, such as some types of eczema. Once again, you don't have to miss out as there are muffins that are completely dairy-free and utterly scrumptious.

Of course, eating well is not just a case of going without things. Try the High-Energy Muffins (see page 40) for breakfast and put a real spring in your step. Nutritionists regard this as the most important meal of the day, but it tends to be the one we most often ignore or skip. Starting off the day with an energy-enhancing boost is not only sensible but also a pleasure.

MAKES 10
280 g/10 oz self-raising wholemeal
    flour
2 tsp baking powder
2 tbsp dark muscovado sugar
100 g/3½ oz ready-to-eat dried
    apricots, finely chopped
1 banana, mashed with
    1 tbsp orange juice

1 tsp finely grated orange rind
300 ml/10 fl oz skimmed milk
1 egg, beaten
3 tbsp sunflower oil
2 tbsp rolled oats
fruit spread, honey or maple syrup,
    to serve

Fruity Muffins

If you like dried figs, they make a deliciously crunchy alternative to the apricots; they also go very well with the flavour of orange. Other ready-to-eat dried fruit, chopped finely, can be used as well.

• Preheat the oven to 200°C/400°F/Gas Mark 6. Place 10 muffin paper cases in a muffin tin.
• Sift the flour and baking powder into a mixing bowl, adding any husks that remain in the sieve. Stir in the sugar and chopped apricots.
• Make a well in the centre and add the banana, orange rind, milk, beaten egg and oil. Mix together well to form a thick batter and divide among the muffin cases.
• Sprinkle with a few rolled oats and bake in the oven for 25–30 minutes until well risen and firm to the touch or until a cocktail stick inserted into the centre comes out clean.
• Remove the muffins from the oven and put them on a wire rack to cool slightly. Serve the muffins while still warm with a little fruit spread, honey or maple syrup.

MAKES 18

butter, for greasing

225 g/8 oz plain flour

2 tsp baking powder

½ tsp salt

50 g/1¾ oz caster sugar

55 g/2 oz butter, melted

2 eggs, lightly beaten

175 ml/6 fl oz milk

115 g/4 oz fresh cranberries

50 g/1¾ oz freshly grated
     Parmesan cheese

Cranberry Muffins

For a sweeter alternative, replace the Parmesan cheese with demerara sugar.

• Preheat the oven to 200°C/400°F/Gas Mark 6. Lightly grease 2 x 9-cup muffin tins with butter.
• Sift the flour, baking powder and salt into a mixing bowl. Stir in the caster sugar.
• In a separate bowl, combine the melted butter, beaten eggs and milk, then pour into the bowl of dry ingredients. Mix lightly together until all of the ingredients are evenly combined, then stir in the fresh cranberries.
• Divide the mixture between the prepared 18 cups in the muffin tins (they should be about two-thirds full). Sprinkle the grated Parmesan cheese over the top.
• Bake in the oven for about 20 minutes or until the muffins are well risen and a golden brown colour.
• Remove the muffins from the oven and leave to cool slightly in the tins. Put the muffins on a wire rack and leave to cool completely.

MAKES 12
butter, for greasing
175 g/6 oz floury potatoes, diced
125 g/4½ oz self-raising flour

2 tbsp soft brown sugar
1 tsp baking powder
140 g/5 oz raisins
4 eggs, separated

Potato and Raisin Muffins

Instead of spreading the muffins with plain butter, serve them with cinnamon butter made by blending 5 tablespoons of butter with a large pinch of ground cinnamon.

• Preheat the oven to 200°C/400°F/Gas Mark 6. Lightly grease a 12-cup muffin tin.
• Cook the diced potatoes in a saucepan of boiling water for 10 minutes, or until tender. Drain well and mash until smooth.
• Transfer the mashed potatoes to a mixing bowl and add the flour, sugar, baking powder, raisins and egg yolks. Stir well to mix thoroughly.
• In a clean, grease-free bowl, whisk the egg whites until they are standing in peaks. Using a metal spoon, gently fold them into the potato mixture until fully incorporated.
• Divide the mixture between the prepared tins (they should be about two-thirds full). Cook the muffins in the oven for 10 minutes. Reduce the oven temperature to 160°C/325°F/Gas Mark 3 and cook the muffins for a further 7–10 minutes or until risen.
• Remove the muffins from the oven and serve warm, buttered, if you like.

MAKES 12

1 large cooking apple, peeled, cored
    and thinly sliced

3 tbsp water

1 tsp mixed spice

2 tbsp vegetable oil, plus extra for
    oiling (if using)

215 g/7½ oz plain white or
    wholemeal flour

1 tbsp baking powder

¼ tsp salt

50 g/1¾ oz wheatgerm

60 g/2¼ oz fresh raspberries

60 g/2¼ oz fresh strawberries, hulled
    and chopped

6 tbsp maple syrup

175 ml/6 fl oz apple juice

Dairy-free Berry Muffins

To make a richer muffin, you can replace the apple juice with the same quantity of soya milk. You can also vary the spices: try using cinnamon or nutmeg instead of the mixed spice.

• Put the sliced cooking apple and water into a saucepan and bring to the boil. Reduce the heat, stir in half of the mixed spice, cover the pan and simmer, stirring occasionally, for 15–20 minutes until the water has been absorbed. Remove from the heat and leave to cool. Transfer to a food processor and blend until smooth.

• Preheat the oven to 190°C/375°F/Gas Mark 5. Oil a 12-cup muffin tin with a little vegetable oil, or line it with muffin paper cases.

• Sift the flour, baking powder, salt and remaining mixed spice into a mixing bowl. Then stir in the wheatgerm.

• In a separate bowl, mix together the raspberries, chopped strawberries, maple syrup, remaining oil, puréed apple and the apple juice. Add the fruit mixture to the flour mixture and then gently stir together until just combined. Do not over-stir the mixture – it is fine for it to be a little lumpy.

• Divide the mixture between the 12 cups in the muffin tin or the paper cases (they should be about two-thirds full). Transfer to the oven and bake for about 25 minutes or until risen and golden. Remove the muffins from the oven and serve warm, or put them on a wire rack and leave to cool.

MAKES 12

5 tbsp vegetable oil, plus extra for
    oiling (if using)
75 g/2¾ oz wholemeal flour
40 g/1½ oz quick-cooking oats
50 g/1¾ oz wheatgerm
2 tsp baking powder
1 tsp ground cinnamon
¼ tsp salt

55 g/2 oz ready-to-eat dried dates,
    stoned and chopped
55 g/2 oz sultanas
140 g/5 oz bran flakes
200 ml/7 fl oz milk
2 eggs, beaten
5 tbsp clear honey
4 tbsp golden syrup
4 tbsp treacle

High-energy Muffins

These muffins are packed with fast-acting and slow-release carbohydrates, and are therefore great for people who need lots of energy, such as athletes. You can vary the fruit to your taste. For example, try using the same quantity of dried chopped apricots instead of the dates. You can also add a small, ripe, mashed banana to the fruit for extra energy and flavour.

• Preheat the oven to 190°C/375°F/Gas Mark 5. Oil a 12-cup muffin tin with vegetable oil, or line it with muffin paper cases.
• Put the flour, oats, wheatgerm, baking powder, cinnamon and salt into a mixing bowl and mix together.
• In a separate bowl, mix together the dates, sultanas and bran flakes. Pour in the milk and stir together. Then stir in the beaten eggs, honey, golden syrup, treacle and remaining oil. Add the fruit mixture to the flour mixture and then gently stir together until just combined. Do not over-stir the mixture – it is fine for it to be a little lumpy.
• Divide the mixture between the 12 cups in the muffin tin or the paper cases (they should be about two-thirds full). Transfer to the oven and bake for 20–25 minutes or until risen and golden. Remove the muffins from the oven and serve warm, or put them on a wire rack and leave to cool.

MAKES 12

4 tbsp vegetable oil, plus extra for
   oiling (if using)
225 g/8 oz plain flour
1 tbsp baking powder
1 tbsp cocoa powder
½ tsp mixed spice

2 eggs
175 ml/6 fl oz unsweetened
   orange juice
1 tsp grated orange rind
100 g/3½ oz fresh blueberries

Sugarless Chocolate Muffins

For a really deep chocolate experience, you can add 90g/3¼ oz sugar-free chocolate chips to this recipe. If you can't find sugar-free chocolate chips in your local shops, you can use a sugar-free chocolate bar instead. Simply cut off 90 g/3¼ oz of chocolate, then chop it into smaller pieces. Gently stir them into the mixture just before dividing it among the paper cases or muffin cups, then bake in the usual way.

• Preheat the oven to 200°C/400°F/Gas Mark 6. Oil a 12-cup muffin tin with vegetable oil, or line it with muffin paper cases.

• Sift the flour, baking powder, cocoa powder and mixed spice into a large mixing bowl.

• In a separate bowl, whisk together the eggs with the remaining oil. Pour in the orange juice, add the grated orange rind and the blueberries and stir together gently to mix. Add the egg and fruit mixture to the flour mixture and then gently stir together until just combined. Do not over-stir the mixture – it is fine for it to be a little lumpy.

• Divide the mixture between the 12 cups in the muffin tin or the paper cases (they should be about two-thirds full). Transfer to the oven and bake for about 20 minutes or until risen and golden. Remove the muffins from the oven and serve warm, or put them on a wire rack and leave to cool.

MAKES 12
215 g/7½ oz plain flour
2 tsp baking powder
¼ tsp salt
½ tsp mixed spice
5 tbsp caster sugar

2 egg whites
2 ripe bananas, sliced
75 g/2¾ oz ready-to-eat dried dates,
    stoned and chopped
4 tbsp skimmed milk
5 tbsp maple syrup

Low-fat Banana and Date Muffins

This recipe is excellent for people on a low-fat diet. It also works well without the dates. You can replace the dates with the same quantity of chopped dried figs or apricots.

• Preheat the oven to 200°C/400°F/Gas Mark 6. Line a 12-cup muffin tin with muffin paper cases.

• Sift the flour, baking powder, salt and mixed spice into a mixing bowl. Add the caster sugar and mix together.

• In a separate bowl, whisk together the egg whites. Mash the sliced bananas in another bowl, then add them to the egg whites. Add the dates, then pour in the skimmed milk and maple syrup and stir together gently to mix. Add the banana and date mixture to the flour mixture and then gently stir together until just combined. Do not over-stir the mixture — it is fine for it to be a little lumpy.

• Divide the mixture between the paper cases (they should be about two-thirds full). Transfer to the oven and bake for about 25 minutes or until risen and golden. Remove the muffins from the oven and serve warm, or put them on a wire rack and leave to cool.

MAKES 12
225 g/8 oz plain flour
1 tsp bicarbonate of soda
¼ tsp salt
1 tsp mixed spice
115 g/4 oz caster sugar

3 egg whites
3 tbsp low-fat margarine
150 ml/5 fl oz thick, low-fat, natural or
  blueberry-flavoured yogurt
1 tsp vanilla essence
115 g/4 oz fresh blueberries

Low-fat Blueberry Muffins

Another way to test that your muffins are cooked is to remove them from the oven at the end of the cooking time and insert a toothpick into the centre of one of the muffins. If it comes out clean, the muffins are cooked. If it does not come out clean, then return the muffins to the oven and bake for a little longer.

• Preheat the oven to 190°C/375°F/Gas Mark 5. Line a 12-cup muffin tin with muffin paper cases.
• Sift the flour, bicarbonate of soda, salt and half of the mixed spice into a large mixing bowl. Add 6 tablespoons of the caster sugar and mix together.
• In a separate bowl, whisk together the egg whites. Add the margarine, yogurt and vanilla essence and mix together well, then stir in the fresh blueberries until thoroughly mixed. Add the fruit mixture to the flour mixture and then gently stir together until just combined. Do not over-stir the mixture – it is fine for it to be a little lumpy.
• Divide the mixture between the paper cases (they should be about two-thirds full). Mix the remaining sugar with the remaining mixed spice, then sprinkle the mixture over the muffins. Transfer to the oven and bake for about 25 minutes or until risen and golden. Remove the muffins from the oven and serve warm, or put them on a wire rack and leave to cool.

MAKES 12

2 tbsp vegetable oil, plus extra for
    oiling (if using)
100 g/3½ oz plain flour
100 g/3½ oz wholemeal flour
1 tsp bicarbonate of soda
¼ tsp salt
1 tsp ground cinnamon
½ tsp ground ginger

2 tbsp caster sugar
2 egg whites
5 tbsp skimmed or semi-skimmed milk
225 g/8 oz canned pineapple chunks
    in juice, drained and chopped
250 g/9 oz carrots, grated
40 g/1½ oz sultanas
40 g/1½ oz walnuts, chopped

TOPPING
250 g/9 oz Quark
    (or any low-fat soft cheese)
1½ tbsp caster sugar
1½ tsp vanilla essence
1½ tsp ground cinnamon

Spiced Carrot Cake Muffins

If you are catering for a party, why not spoon the mixture into mini-muffin tins instead? The mixture will go a lot further and will create an abundance of mouth-watering morsels that will look good on any party buffet table.

• Preheat the oven to 190°C/375°F/Gas Mark 5. Oil a 12-cup muffin tin with vegetable oil, or line it with muffin paper cases.

• Sift the plain flour, wholemeal flour, bicarbonate of soda, salt, cinnamon and ginger into a mixing bowl. Add the caster sugar and mix together.

• In a separate bowl, whisk together the egg whites, then pour in the milk and remaining oil and mix together. Mash the pineapple chunks, then add to the egg mixture. Add the carrots, sultanas and walnuts and stir together gently. Add the fruit mixture to the flour mixture and then gently stir together until just combined. Do not over-stir the mixture – it is fine for it to be a little lumpy.

• Divide the mixture evenly between the 12 cups in the muffin tin or the paper cases (they should be about two-thirds full). Transfer to the oven and bake for about 25 minutes or until risen and golden.

• While the muffins are in the oven, make the topping. Put the Quark into a mixing bowl with the caster sugar, vanilla essence and 1 teaspoon of the cinnamon. Mix together well, then cover with clingfilm and transfer to the refrigerator until ready to use.

• When the muffins are cooked, remove them from the oven, put them on a wire rack and leave to cool. When they have cooled to room temperature, remove the topping from the refrigerator and spread some evenly over the top of each muffin. Lightly sprinkle over the remaining cinnamon and serve.

MAKES 12
3 large cooking apples, peeled and
    cored
475 ml/13 fl oz water
1½ tsp mixed spice

280 g/10 oz wholemeal flour
1 tbsp baking powder
¼ tsp salt
3 tbsp caster sugar
125 g/4½ oz fresh raspberries

Low-fat Apple and Raspberry Muffins

These delicious muffins are extremely low in fat and ideal for a low-fat diet. You can also vary the amount of sugar according to your taste. Try reducing the amount to 2 tablespoons for less sweetness, or increase it to 4 tablespoons for sweeter muffins.

• Thinly slice 2 cooking apples and put them into a saucepan with 6 tablespoons of the water. Bring to the boil, then reduce the heat, stir in ½ teaspoon of the mixed spice, cover the saucepan and simmer, stirring occasionally, for 15–20 minutes until the water has been absorbed. Remove from the heat and leave to cool. Transfer to a food processor and blend until smooth. Stir in the remaining water and mix well.

• Preheat the oven to 200°C/400°F/Gas Mark 6. Line a 12-cup muffin tin with muffin paper cases. Sift the flour, baking powder, salt and remaining mixed spice into a mixing bowl. Then stir in the sugar.

• Chop the remaining apple and add to the flour mixture. Add the raspberries, then combine gently with the flour mixture until lightly coated. Finally, gently stir in the cooled apple/water mixture. Do not over-stir the mixture – it is fine for it to be a little lumpy.

• Divide the mixture evenly between the paper cases (they should be about two-thirds full). Transfer to the oven and bake for about 25 minutes or until risen and golden. Remove the muffins from the oven and serve warm, or put them on a wire rack and leave to cool.

For a novel approach to party nibbles, these delightful little savouries can be served warm from the oven or, if made in advance simply reheated. For picnics and school lunch boxes, Saturday brunch for family and friends or even an after-theatre or post-movie evening snack, there are few things more appetizing and tempting than savoury muffins. They're also the perfect choice, perhaps served with a steaming bowl of soup, on a cold winter's evening when you don't feel much like cooking and just want to snuggle on the sofa and watch your favourite soap. They are delicious served warm or cold and are just as quick and easy to make as their better-known sweet counterparts. Most people are familiar with the idea of cheese muffins — and there are some terrific recipes for these in this chapter — but the range of other flavours may well surprise you.

SAVOURY MUFFINS

Peckish meat-lovers are guaranteed to enjoy Spicy Chicken Muffins (see page 66) or Potato and Pancetta Muffins (see page 72), while fans of seafood will find Crab and Cream Cheese Muffins (see page 64) simply irresistible. Nor are the vegetarian choices limited to cheese. Try Italian Tomato Muffins (see page 56) or Soured Cream Muffins with Chives (see page 58).

Savoury muffins are also a great choice for breakfast, providing an energizing start to the day. More fun and more nourishing than cereals, they are also sure to be popular with all the family and are a good way to ring the changes without lots of extra effort. Everyone is certain to put their best foot forward when facing the day ahead if they've stoked up on freshly baked Pancetta and Polenta Muffins (see page 70) or Herb Muffins with Smoked Cheese (see page 60) before leaving the house.

MAKES 10

115 g/4 oz self-raising flour

1 tbsp baking powder

1 tsp salt

225 g/8 oz fine polenta

150 g/5½ oz grated mature Cheddar
    cheese

55 g/2 oz butter, melted

2 eggs, beaten

1 garlic clove, crushed

300 ml/10 fl oz milk

Cheese Muffins

Polenta, or cornmeal, used to be difficult to find, but it is now widely available in most major supermarkets and health-food shops.

• Preheat the oven to 200°C/400°F/Gas Mark 6. Line 10 cups of a 12-cup muffin tin with paper muffin cases.

• Sift the flour, baking powder and salt into a bowl, then stir in the polenta and 115 g/4 oz of the cheese.

• Place the melted butter, eggs, crushed garlic and milk in a separate bowl. Add the wet ingredients to the dry ingredients and mix gently until just combined.

• Divide the mixture between the paper cases (they should be about two-thirds full). Sprinkle over the remaining cheese and bake in the oven for 20–25 minutes or until risen and golden brown. Remove the muffins from the oven and serve warm, or put on a wire rack and leave to cool.

MAKES 12
300 g/10½ oz Italian plum tomatoes
140 g/5 oz plain flour
2 tbsp baking powder
½ tsp salt
200 g/7 oz fine polenta

1 egg, lightly beaten
300 ml/10 fl oz milk
1 garlic clove, crushed
1 tbsp chopped fresh basil
1½ tsp chopped fresh parsley

Italian Tomato Muffins

To peel tomatoes, bring a kettle of water to a boil. Place the tomatoes in a heatproof bowl, then pour over enough boiling water to cover them. Let them soak for about 3 minutes, then lift them out of the water and let cool slightly. When the tomatoes are cool enough to handle, gently pierce the skins with the tip of a knife. Remove and discard the skins.

• First peel the tomatoes (see left), then deseed them (use a teaspoon for this). Chop the tomatoes finely and set aside.
• Preheat the oven to 200°C/400°F/Gas Mark 6. Line a 12-cup muffin tin with muffin paper cases.
• Sift the flour, baking powder and salt into a large mixing bowl. Then add the polenta and mix together well.
• In a separate bowl, lightly whisk together the egg and the milk with a fork. Add the reserved chopped tomatoes, then the garlic, basil and parsley and mix together well. Add the egg and tomato mixture to the flour mixture and then gently stir together until just combined. Do not over-stir the mixture – it is fine for it to be a little lumpy.
• Divide the mixture between the paper cases (they should be about two-thirds full). Transfer to the oven and bake for about 20 minutes or until risen and golden. Remove the muffins from the oven and serve warm, or put them on a wire rack and leave to cool.

MAKES 12

1 tbsp vegetable oil, for oiling
  (if using)

280 g/10 oz plain flour

2 tsp baking powder

½ tsp bicarbonate of soda

25 g/1 oz Cheddar cheese, grated

35 g/1¼ oz fresh chives, finely
  snipped, plus extra to garnish

1 egg, lightly beaten

200 ml/7 fl oz soured cream

100 ml/3½ fl oz natural
  unsweetened yogurt

55 g/2 oz butter, melted

Sour Cream Muffins with Chives

These muffins are deliciously creamy and a real treat for any picnic, buffet or lunch box. For extra flavour, try stirring 2 tablespoons finely chopped spring onion into the mixture when you add the chives.

• Preheat the oven to 200°C/400°F/Gas Mark 6. Oil a 12-cup muffin tin with vegetable oil, or line it with muffin paper cases. Sift the flour, baking powder and bicarbonate of soda into a large mixing bowl. Add the cheese and chives and mix together well.

• In a separate bowl, lightly mix together the egg, soured cream, yogurt and melted butter. Add the soured cream mixture to the flour mixture and then gently stir together until just combined. Do not over-stir the mixture — it is fine for it to be a little lumpy.

• Divide the mixture between the 12 cups in the muffin tin or the paper cases (they should be about two-thirds full). Sprinkle over the remaining snipped chives to garnish and transfer to the oven. Bake for about 20 minutes or until risen and golden. Remove the muffins from the oven and serve warm, or put them on a wire rack and leave to cool.

MAKES 12
280 g/10 oz plain flour
2 tsp baking powder
½ tsp bicarbonate of soda
25 g/1 oz smoked hard cheese,
    such as Applewood, grated

50 g/1¾ oz fresh parsley,
    finely chopped
1 egg, lightly beaten
300 ml/10 fl oz thick Greek-style
    natural yogurt
55 g/2 oz butter, melted

Herb Muffins with Smoked Cheese

The smoked cheese gives these muffins a wonderfully smoky flavour. If smoked cheese is unavailable, however, you can replace it with the same quantity of ordinary mature Cheddar cheese.

• Preheat the oven to 200°C/400°F/Gas Mark 6. Line a 12-cup muffin tin with muffin paper cases.
• Sift the flour, baking powder and bicarbonate of soda into a large mixing bowl. Add the smoked cheese and the parsley and mix together well.
• In a separate bowl, lightly mix together the egg, yogurt and melted butter. Add the yogurt mixture to the flour mixture and then gently stir together until just combined. Do not over-stir the mixture – it is fine for it to be a little lumpy.
• Divide the mixture between the paper cases (they should be about two-thirds full), then transfer to the oven. Bake for about 20 minutes or until risen and golden. Remove the muffins from the oven and serve warm, or put them on a wire rack and leave to cool.

MAKES 12
150 ml/5 fl oz vegetable oil, plus extra
     for oiling (if using)
280 g/10 oz plain flour
1 tbsp baking powder
1/2 tsp salt

3 tbsp granulated sugar
2 eggs
175 ml/6 fl oz milk
400 g/14 oz courgettes, shredded
25 g/1 oz Manchego cheese, grated
2 tbsp chopped fresh flat-leaf parsley

Spanish Manchego Muffins

To ring the changes, try varying the flavour by replacing the chopped parsley with the same quantity of other chopped fresh herbs, such as oregano, rosemary or basil.

• Preheat the oven to 200°C/400°F/Gas Mark 6. Oil a 12-cup muffin tin with vegetable oil, or line it with muffin paper cases.
• Sift the flour, baking powder and salt into a large mixing bowl. Add the sugar and mix together well.
• In a separate bowl, lightly beat the eggs. Stir in the milk and remaining vegetable oil and mix together. Add the egg mixture to the flour mixture and then gently stir together. Gently stir in the courgettes, Manchego cheese and chopped parsley until just combined. Do not over-stir the mixture — it is fine for it to be a little lumpy.
• Divide the mixture between the 12 cups in the muffin tin or the paper cases (they should be about two-thirds full), then transfer to the oven. Bake for about 25 minutes or until risen and golden. Remove the muffins from the oven and serve warm, or put them on a wire rack and leave to cool.

MAKES 12

1 tbsp vegetable oil, for greasing
   (if using)
280 g/10 oz plain flour
1½ tsp baking powder
½ tsp bicarbonate of soda
½ tsp salt

1 egg
150 ml/5 fl oz natural yogurt
150 ml/5 fl oz soured cream
25 g/1 oz Cheddar cheese, grated
25 g/1 oz chopped fresh parsley
25 g/1 oz chopped fresh dill

CRAB AND CREAM CHEESE FILLING
200 g/7 oz canned crabmeat, drained
200 g/7 oz cream cheese
2 tbsp mayonnaise
salt and pepper

Crab and Cream Cheese Muffins

For a salmon filling, replace the canned crabmeat with the same quantity of canned salmon, and stir in 1 tablespoon chopped fresh dill. For a tuna filling, replace the crabmeat with the same quantity of canned tuna, and stir in 4 tbsp canned sweetcorn.

• Preheat the oven to 200°C/400°F/Gas Mark 6. Oil a 12-cup muffin tin with vegetable oil, or line it with muffin paper cases.
• Sift the flour, baking powder, bicarbonate of soda and salt into a large mixing bowl.
• In a separate bowl, lightly beat the egg, then pour in the yogurt and soured cream and mix together. Stir in the grated cheese and chopped herbs. Add the soured cream and cheese mixture to the flour mixture, then gently stir together. Do not over-stir the mixture — it is fine for it to be a little lumpy.
• Divide the mixture between the 12 cups in the muffin tin or the paper cases (they should be about two-thirds full), then transfer to the oven. Bake for about 20 minutes or until risen and golden.
• While the muffins are cooking, make the crab and cream cheese filling. Put the crabmeat into a mixing bowl and flake with a fork. Add the cream cheese and mayonnaise and mix together well. Season to taste with salt and pepper. Cover the bowl with clingfilm and chill in the refrigerator until ready for use.
• When the muffins are cooked, remove them from the oven, put them on a wire rack and leave to cool to room temperature. When they have cooled, cut them in half horizontally. Remove the crabmeat filling from the refrigerator and spread it over the bottom halves of the muffins. Replace the top halves so that the filling is sandwiched in the middle, and serve.

MAKES 12

125 ml/4 fl oz vegetable oil,
    plus extra for oiling

2 onions, chopped

3 spring onions, chopped

1 small fresh red chilli, deseeded and
    finely chopped

3 skinless, boneless chicken thighs,
    chopped

1 tsp paprika

315 g/11 oz self-raising flour

1 tsp baking powder

2 eggs

1 tbsp lemon juice

1 tbsp grated lemon rind

125 ml/4 fl oz soured cream

125 ml/4 fl oz natural yogurt

Spicy Chicken Muffins

These muffins can be served warm, but they are also good served cold in lunch boxes and on picnics. If you haven't got a fresh red chilli, simply omit it and replace the paprika with 1 teaspoon of mild chilli powder.

• Preheat the oven to 190°C/375°F/Gas Mark 5. Oil a 12-cup muffin tin with vegetable oil, or line it with muffin paper cases.

• Heat a little of the vegetable oil in a frying pan, add the onions, spring onions and chilli and cook over a low heat, stirring constantly, for 3 minutes. Remove from the heat, lift out the onions and chilli and set aside. Heat a little more vegetable oil in the frying pan, add the chicken and paprika, and cook, stirring, over a medium heat for 5 minutes. Remove from the heat and set aside.

• Sift the flour and baking powder into a large mixing bowl. In a separate bowl, lightly beat the eggs, then stir in the remaining vegetable oil and the lemon juice and rind. Pour in the soured cream and the yogurt and mix together. Add the egg mixture to the flour mixture, then gently stir in the onions, spring onions, chilli and chicken. Do not over-stir the mixture – it is fine for it to be a little lumpy.

• Divide the mixture between the 12 cups in the muffin tin or the paper cases (they should be about two-thirds full), then transfer to the oven. Bake for approximately 20 minutes or until risen about golden. Remove the muffins from the oven and serve warm, or put them on a wire rack and leave to cool.

MAKES 12

2 tbsp vegetable oil, plus extra for
  oiling (if using)

1 leek, trimmed and finely chopped

280 g/10 oz plain flour

2 tsp baking powder

½ tsp bicarbonate of soda

1 egg, lightly beaten

300 ml/10 fl oz thick Greek-style
  natural yogurt

55 g/2 oz butter, melted

25 g/1 oz Cheddar cheese, grated

25 g/1 oz fresh chives, finely snipped

150 g/5½ oz cooked ham, chopped

Savoury Leek and Ham Muffins

Cooked bacon works as well as ham in these muffins. You can also replace some or all of the Cheddar cheese with a smoked cheese, such as Applewood, for an added smoky flavour.

• Preheat the oven to 200°C/400°F/Gas Mark 6. Oil a 12-cup muffin tin with vegetable oil, or line it with muffin paper cases.
• Heat the remaining vegetable oil in a frying pan, add the chopped leek, and cook, stirring, over a low heat for 2 minutes. Remove from the heat and leave to cool.
• Sift the flour, baking powder and bicarbonate of soda into a large mixing bowl. In a separate bowl, lightly mix together the egg, yogurt and melted butter. Add the Cheddar cheese, chives, cooked leek and half of the chopped ham, then mix together well. Add the cheese mixture to the flour mixture and then gently stir together until just combined. Do not over-stir the mixture – it is fine for it to be a little lumpy.
• Divide the mixture between the 12 cups in the muffin tin or the paper cases (they should be about two-thirds full). Sprinkle over the remaining chopped ham, then transfer to the oven. Bake for about 20 minutes or until risen and golden. Remove the muffins from the oven and serve warm, or put them on a wire rack and then leave to cool.

MAKES 12

150 g/5½ oz pancetta

150 g/5½ oz self-raising flour

1 tbsp baking powder

1 tsp salt

250 g/9 oz fine polenta

55 g/2 oz golden granulated sugar

100 g/3½ oz butter, melted

2 eggs, beaten

300 ml/10 fl oz milk

Pancetta and Polenta Muffins

Pancetta is thin Italian bacon. If it is unavailable, you can use thinly sliced rashers of streaky bacon instead.

• Preheat the oven to 200°C/400°F/Gas Mark 6 and preheat the grill to medium. Line a 12-cup muffin tin with paper muffin cases.

• Cook the pancetta under the preheated grill until crisp and then crumble into pieces. Reserve until required.

• Sift the flour, baking powder and salt into a bowl, then stir in the polenta and sugar. Place the butter, eggs and milk in a separate bowl. Add the wet ingredients to the dry ingredients and mix until just blended.

• Fold in the crumbled pancetta, then divide the mixture between the paper cases (they should be about two-thirds full) and bake in the oven for 20–25 minutes or until risen and golden. Remove the muffins from the oven and serve warm, or put them on a wire rack and leave to cool.

MAKES 12

1 tbsp vegetable oil, plus extra for
    greasing (if using)
3 shallots, finely chopped
350 g/12 oz self-raising flour
1 tsp salt
450 g/1 lb potatoes, cooked and
    mashed

2 eggs
350 ml/12 fl oz milk
125 ml/4 fl oz soured cream
1 tbsp finely snipped fresh chives
150 g/5½ oz pancetta, chopped
4 tbsp grated Red Leicester or
    Cheddar cheese

Potato and Pancetta Muffins

To make a lower-fat version of these muffins, use muffin paper cases and cook the shallots in vegetable-oil spray instead of vegetable oil. Use semi-skimmed or skimmed milk instead of full-fat milk, and replace the soured cream with the same quantity of Greek-style thick natural yogurt. Finally, use a low-fat Red Leicester or Cheddar cheese, or omit the cheese altogether.

• Preheat the oven to 200°C/400°F/Gas Mark 6. Oil a 12-cup muffin tin with vegetable oil, or line it with muffin paper cases. Heat the remaining vegetable oil in a frying pan, add the chopped shallots and cook, stirring, over a low heat for 2 minutes. Remove from the heat and leave to cool.

• Sift the flour and salt into a large mixing bowl. In a separate bowl, mix together the mashed potato, eggs, milk, soured cream, chives and half of the pancetta. Add the potato mixture to the flour mixture and then gently stir together until just combined. Do not over-stir the mixture – it is fine for it to be a little lumpy.

• Divide the mixture between the 12 cups in the muffin tin or the paper cases (they should be about two-thirds full). Sprinkle over the remaining chopped pancetta, then sprinkle over the grated cheese. Transfer to the oven and bake for about 20 minutes, or until risen and golden. Remove the muffins from the oven and serve warm, or put them on a wire rack and leave to cool.

A celebration tea party, a fund-raising coffee morning, a Mother's Day breakfast in bed, stocking the cake stall at the school summer fair — these are just some of the reasons why you might want to the push the boat out with this mouth-watering collection of extra special muffins. In fact, baking a batch of these superb tempting treats will turn any occasion into a special one. If you can bear to part with them, you could even pack them into a pretty box to make a charming gift.

Some of these recipes are strictly for adults only. Rice Muffins with Amaretto (see page 76) are served with an almond-flavoured liqueur butter and the mildly laced Irish Coffee Muffins (see page 88) and Apricot Muffins with Cointreau (see page 90) speak for themselves.

SPECIAL OCCASIONS

The wickedly indulgent Triple Chocolate Muffins (see page 78), on the other hand, will appeal to chocoholics of all ages, while Marshmallow Muffins (see page 80) appear to have a totally irresistible fascination for anyone under the age of twelve.

Sweetly scented cakes flavoured with edible flowers, such as Iced Lavender Muffins (see page 84), make a stylish addition to the tea table redolent of a more gracious age of silver services, porcelain cups, crisp linen and rolling country house lawns, while Mocha Muffins (see page 94) are just designed for a cosy, gossipy coffee morning with the neighbours. But, in fact, you don't need an excuse to enjoy these fabulous confections — simply making them in the first place is celebration enough.

MAKES 9
butter, for greasing
140 g/5 oz plain flour
1 tbsp baking powder
½ tsp bicarbonate of soda
½ tsp salt
1 egg

4 tbsp clear honey
125 ml/4 fl oz milk
2 tbsp sunflower oil
½ tsp almond essence
175 g/6 oz cooked risotto rice
2–3 amaretti, coarsely crushed

AMARETTO BUTTER
115 g/4 oz unsalted butter,
    at room temperature
1 tbsp clear honey
1–2 tbsp Amaretto
1–2 tbsp mascarpone cheese

Rice Muffins with Amaretto

Italian rice gives these delicate muffins an interesting texture. The amaretti biscuits complement the flavour and add a crunchy topping.

• Preheat the oven to 200°C/400°F/Gas Mark 6. Grease 9 cups of a 12-cup muffin tin or 2 x 6-cup tins.

• Sift the flour, baking powder, bicarbonate of soda and salt into a large bowl and stir. Make a well in the centre.

• In another bowl, beat the egg, honey, milk, oil and almond essence with an electric whisk for about 2 minutes, or until light and foamy. Gradually beat in the rice. Pour into the well and, using a fork, stir lightly until just combined. Do not beat too long or the mixture can become lumpy.

• Divide the mixture between the 9 cups in the muffin tin (they should be about two-thirds full). Sprinkle each with some of the amaretti crumbs and bake for 15 minutes until risen and golden. The tops should spring back when pressed. Remove from the oven and cool in the tin for about 1 minute. Carefully remove the muffins and leave to cool slightly.

• To make the Amaretto butter, put the butter and honey in a small bowl and beat until creamy. Add the Amaretto and mascarpone and beat together. Spoon into a small serving bowl and serve with the warm muffins.

MAKES 12
250 g/9 oz plain flour
25 g/1 oz cocoa powder
2 tsp baking powder
½ tsp bicarbonate of soda
100 g/3½ oz plain chocolate chips

100 g/3½ oz white chocolate chips
2 eggs, beaten
300 ml/10 fl oz soured cream
85 g/3 oz light muscovado sugar
85 g/3 oz butter, melted

Triple Chocolate Muffins

Packed with melting plain and white chocolate, these creamy muffins are a chocoholic's delight. Serve with coffee for a real treat.

• Preheat the oven to 200°C/400°F/Gas Mark 6. Line a 12-cup muffin tin with muffin paper cases.
• Sift the flour, cocoa, baking powder and bicarbonate of soda into a large bowl, add the plain and white chocolate chips and stir.
• Place the eggs, soured cream, sugar and melted butter in a separate mixing bowl and mix well. Add the wet ingredients to the dry ingredients and stir gently until just combined.
• Using 2 spoons, divide the mixture between the paper cases and bake in the preheated oven for 20 minutes or until well risen and firm to the touch. Remove from the oven and serve warm, or put on a wire rack and leave to cool.

MAKES 12
70 g/2½ oz butter
280 g/10 oz plain flour
6 tbsp cocoa powder
3 tsp baking powder

85 g/3 oz caster sugar
100 g/3½ oz milk chocolate chips
55 g/2 oz white mini marshmallows
1 egg, beaten
300 ml/10 fl oz milk

Marshmallow Muffins

Don't over-beat the batter (there should still be a few lumps of flour) or the muffins will be crusty.

• Preheat the oven to 190°C/375°F/Gas Mark 5. Place 12 muffin paper cases in a muffin tin.
• Melt the butter. Sift the flour, cocoa and baking powder together into a large bowl. Stir in the sugar, chocolate chips and marshmallows until thoroughly mixed.
• Whisk the egg, milk and melted butter together in a separate bowl, then gently stir into the flour to form a stiff batter. Divide the mixture between the muffin cases (they should be about two-thirds full).
• Bake in the oven for 20–25 minutes until well risen and golden brown. Remove from the oven and leave to cool in the tin for 5 minutes, then put on a wire rack and leave to cool completely.

MAKES 12
250 g/9 oz plain flour
1 tsp baking powder
1 tsp bicarbonate of soda
½ tsp mixed spice
115 g/4 oz butter
200 g/7 oz dark muscovado sugar
2 eggs, beaten

2 tbsp thick natural, banana- or
    pineapple-flavoured yogurt
1 tbsp rum
1 ripe banana, peeled and sliced
75 g/2¾ oz canned pineapple rings,
    drained and chopped
50 g/1¾ oz desiccated coconut

COCONUT TOPPING
4 tbsp demerara sugar
1 tsp mixed spice
25 g/1 oz desiccated coconut

Tropical Coconut Muffins

To make these muffins without the alcohol, perhaps for a children's party, replace the rum with 1 teaspoon almond essence and 2 teaspoons milk.

• Preheat the oven to 200°C/400°F/Gas Mark 6. Line a 12-cup muffin tin with muffin paper cases.

• Sift the flour, baking powder, bicarbonate of soda and mixed spice into a mixing bowl.

• In a separate large bowl, cream together the butter and dark muscovado sugar, then stir in the eggs, yogurt and rum. Add the banana, pineapple and desiccated coconut and mix together gently. Add the pineapple mixture to the flour mixture and then gently stir together until just combined. Do not over-stir the mixture — it is fine for it to be a little lumpy.

• Divide the mixture between the 12 cups in the muffin tin or the paper cases (they should be about two-thirds full). To make the topping, mix together the demerara sugar and mixed spice and sprinkle over the muffins. Sprinkle over the desiccated coconut, then transfer to the preheated oven. Bake for about 20 minutes or until risen and golden. Remove the muffins from the oven and serve warm, or put them on a wire rack and leave to cool.

MAKES 12
1 large cooking apple, peeled,
   cored and thinly sliced
3 tbsp water
140 g/5 oz plain flour
1 tsp baking powder
1 tsp bicarbonate of soda

pinch of salt
55 g/2 oz butter
4 tbsp caster sugar
1 egg, beaten
½ tsp vanilla essence
1 tbsp dried lavender flowers

LAVENDER ICING
100 g/3½ oz icing sugar
1 tbsp dried lavender flowers
1 tbsp liquid glucose
1–2 tbsp milk

Iced Lavender Muffins

To give a deeper colour to these muffins, pour a few drops of liquid lavender food colouring into the icing along with the milk, then stir together well.

• The day before you need to make these muffins, start preparing the icing. Put the icing sugar into a bowl, then add the dried lavender flowers. Cover with clingfilm and leave overnight until ready for use.

• When you are ready to make the muffins, put the sliced cooking apple and water into a saucepan and bring to the boil. Reduce the heat, cover the pan and simmer for 15–20 minutes, stirring occasionally, until the water has been absorbed. Remove from the heat and leave to cool. Transfer to a food processor and process until smooth.

• Preheat the oven to 200°C/400°F/Gas Mark 6. Line a 12-cup muffin tin with muffin paper cases. Sift the flour, baking powder, bicarbonate of soda and salt into a mixing bowl.

• In a separate large bowl, cream together the butter and caster sugar, then stir in the beaten egg, vanilla essence, apple puree and dried lavender flowers, stripped from their stalks. Add the egg mixture to the flour mixture and then gently stir together until just combined. Do not over-stir the mixture – it is fine for it to be a little lumpy.

• Divide the mixture between the paper cases (they should be about two-thirds full). Transfer to the oven and bake for about 20 minutes or until risen and golden.

• While the muffins are cooking, finish making the icing. Remove the clingfilm from the icing sugar/lavender mixture, then sift the mixture into a bowl and discard the lavender flowers. Stir in the liquid glucose and enough milk to make the icing easy to spread. Cover with clingfilm until ready to use.

• When the muffins are cooked, remove them from the oven, put them on a wire rack and leave to cool. When they have cooled completely, spread each muffin with some of the lavender icing and serve.

MAKES 12
215 g/7½ oz plain flour
2 tsp baking powder
pinch of salt
55 g/2 oz butter
6 tbsp caster sugar

1 egg, beaten
125 ml/4 fl oz milk
1 tsp rosewater
50 g/1¾ oz edible rose petals, rinsed,
    patted dry and lightly snipped

ROSE PETAL ICING
100 g/3½ oz icing sugar
1 tbsp liquid glucose
1 tbsp rose water
50 g/1¾ oz edible
    rose petals, rinsed and patted dry

Rose Petal Muffins

You can also make one spectacular large muffin with these ingredients. Put the mixture into a greased 23-cm/9-inch pie dish, then bake in the usual way.

• Preheat the oven to 200°C/400°F/Gas Mark 6. Line a 12-cup muffin tin with muffin paper cases.
• Sift the flour, baking powder and salt into a large mixing bowl.
• In a separate large bowl, cream together the butter and caster sugar, then stir in the beaten egg, milk, rosewater and snipped rose petals. Add the butter mixture to the flour mixture and then gently stir together until just combined. Do not over-stir the mixture – it is fine for it to be a little lumpy.
• Divide the mixture between the paper cases (they should be about two-thirds full). Transfer to the oven and bake for about 20 minutes or until risen and golden.
• While the muffins are cooking, make the icing. Put the icing sugar into a bowl, then stir in the liquid glucose and rosewater. Cover with clingfilm until ready to use.
• When the muffins are cooked, remove them from the oven, put them on a wire rack and leave to cool. When they have cooled, spread each muffin with some of the icing, sprinkle over the snipped rose petals and serve.

MAKES 12
280 g/10 oz plain flour
1 tbsp baking powder
pinch of salt
85 g/3 oz butter
90 g/3¼ oz demerara sugar
1 egg, beaten

125 ml/4 fl oz double cream, plus
    extra for topping
1 tsp almond essence
2 tbsp strong coffee
2 tbsp coffee-flavoured liqueur
4 tbsp Irish whiskey, or similar
    whiskey

Irish Coffee Muffins

For a lower-fat muffin, leave out the filling and replace the double cream with the same quantity of lower-fat single cream.

• Preheat the oven to 200°C/400°F/Gas Mark 6. Line a 12-cup muffin tin with muffin paper cases.
• Sift the flour, baking powder and salt into a large mixing bowl.
• In a separate large bowl, cream together the butter and demerara sugar, then stir in the beaten egg. Pour in the double cream, almond essence, coffee, liqueur and whiskey and stir together. Add the whiskey mixture to the flour mixture and then gently stir together until just combined. Do not over-stir the mixture — it is fine for it to be a little lumpy.
• Divide the mixture between the paper cases (they should be about two-thirds full). Transfer to the oven and bake for about 20 minutes, or until risen and golden. Remove the muffins from the oven and serve warm, or put them on a wire rack and leave to cool. Slice the muffins horizontally across the top and fill with freshly whipped cream.

MAKES 12
125 g/4½ oz self-raising flour
2 tsp baking powder
175 g/6 oz butter
125 g/4½ oz caster sugar
2 large eggs, beaten
125 ml/4 fl oz milk

4 tbsp single cream
1 tbsp orange-flavoured liqueur,
 such as Cointreau
100 g/3½ oz ready-to-eat dried
 apricots, chopped
100 g/3½ oz ready-to-eat dried dates,
 chopped

CINNAMON TOPPING
3 tbsp demerara sugar
1 tsp ground cinnamon
1 tbsp freshly grated orange rind

Apricot Muffins with Cointreau

If you would prefer to make these muffins without the alcohol, replace the orange-flavoured liqueur with 1 tablespoon fresh unsweetened orange juice and 1 tablespoon grated orange rind.

• Preheat the oven to 190°C/375°F/Gas Mark 5. Line a 12-cup muffin tin with muffin paper cases.
• Sift the flour and baking powder into a large mixing bowl.
• In a separate large bowl, cream together the butter and caster sugar, then stir in the beaten eggs. Pour in the milk, cream and orange-flavoured liqueur, then add the chopped apricots and dates and gently mix together. Add the fruit mixture to the flour mixture and then gently stir together until just combined. Do not over-stir the mixture – it is fine for it to be a little lumpy.
• Divide the mixture between the paper cases (they should be about two-thirds full). To make the topping, put the demerara sugar into a small bowl, then mix in the cinnamon and orange rind. Sprinkle the topping over the muffins, then transfer to the oven and bake for about 20 minutes or until risen and golden. Remove the muffins from the oven and serve warm, or put them on a wire rack and then leave to cool.

MAKES 12
225 g/8 oz plain flour
1 tbsp baking powder
pinch of salt
3 tbsp butter
2 tbsp caster sugar

1 egg, beaten
200 ml/7 fl oz milk
2 tsp cherry brandy
300 g/10½ oz drained canned
    cherries, chopped

Brandied Cherry Muffins

These muffins are delicious served with freshly whipped cream (sweetened with a little sugar if necessary) or spoonfuls of fresh mascarpone cheese. Serve the cream or mascarpone alongside the muffins or, for extra decorative flair, allow the muffins to cool, halve them horizontally, then spread the cream or mascarpone over the cut sides of the bases. Top with the other muffin halves, and serve.

• Preheat the oven to 200°C/400°F/Gas Mark 6. Line a 12-cup muffin tin with muffin paper cases.
• Sift the flour, baking powder and salt into a large mixing bowl.
• In a separate large bowl, cream together the butter and caster sugar, then stir in the beaten egg. Pour in the milk and cherry brandy, then add the chopped cherries and gently stir together. Add the cherry mixture to the flour mixture and then gently stir together until just combined. Do not over-stir the mixture – it is fine for it to be a little lumpy.
• Divide the mixture between the paper cases (they should be about two-thirds full). Transfer to the oven and bake for 20–25 minutes or until risen and golden. Remove the muffins from the oven and serve warm, or put them on a wire rack and leave to cool.

MAKES 12
250 g/9 oz plain flour
1 tbsp baking powder
2 tbsp cocoa powder
pinch of salt
115 g/4 oz butter, melted
140 g/5 oz demerara sugar
1 egg, beaten

225 ml/8 fl oz milk
1 tsp almond essence
2 tbsp strong coffee
1 tbsp instant coffee granules
50 g/1¾ oz plain chocolate chips
50 g/1¾ oz raisins

COCOA TOPPING
3 tbsp demerara sugar
1 tbsp cocoa powder
1 tsp mixed spice

Mocha Muffins

To increase the protein content of these muffins and change the flavour and texture, replace the raisins with the same quantity of chopped almonds or walnuts, or use half raisins and half almonds/walnuts.

• Preheat the oven to 190°C/375°F/Gas Mark 5. Line a 12-cup muffin tin with muffin paper cases.
• Sift the flour, baking powder, cocoa powder and salt into a large mixing bowl.
• In a separate large bowl, cream together the melted butter and demerara sugar, then stir in the beaten egg. Pour in the milk, almond essence and coffee, then add the coffee granules, chocolate chips and raisins and gently mix together. Add the raisin mixture to the flour mixture and then gently stir together until just combined. Do not over-stir the mixture – it is fine for it to be a little lumpy.
• Divide the mixture between the paper cases (they should be about two-thirds full). To make the topping, put the demerara sugar into a bowl, add the cocoa powder and mixed spice and mix together well. Sprinkle the topping over the muffins, then transfer to the oven and bake for about 20 minutes or until risen and golden. Remove the muffins from the oven and serve warm, or put them on a wire rack and leave to cool.

Index